Swear Word Coloring Book

Very Rude Cats

SWEAR WORD
ADULT COLORING BOOK

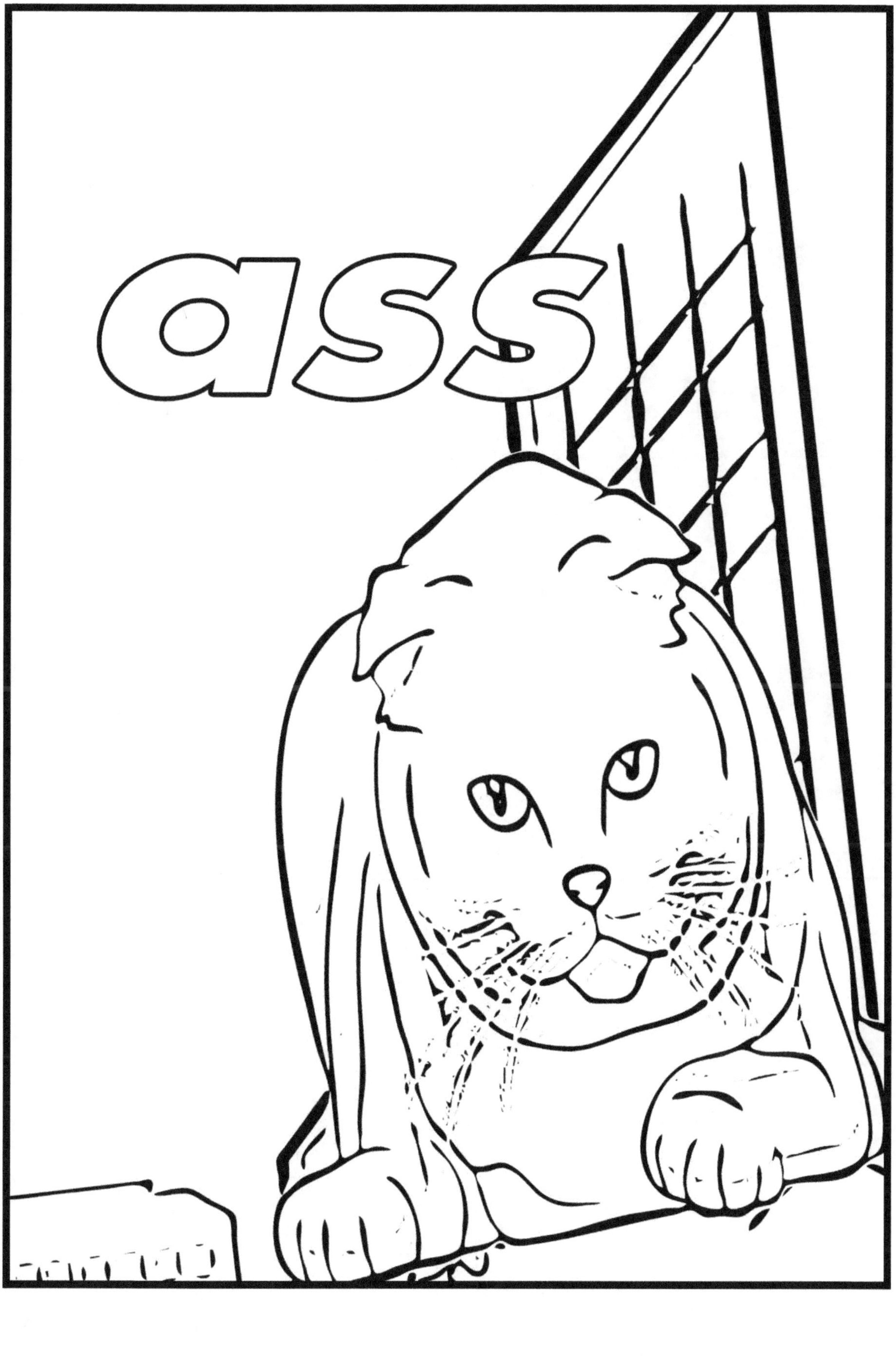
ass

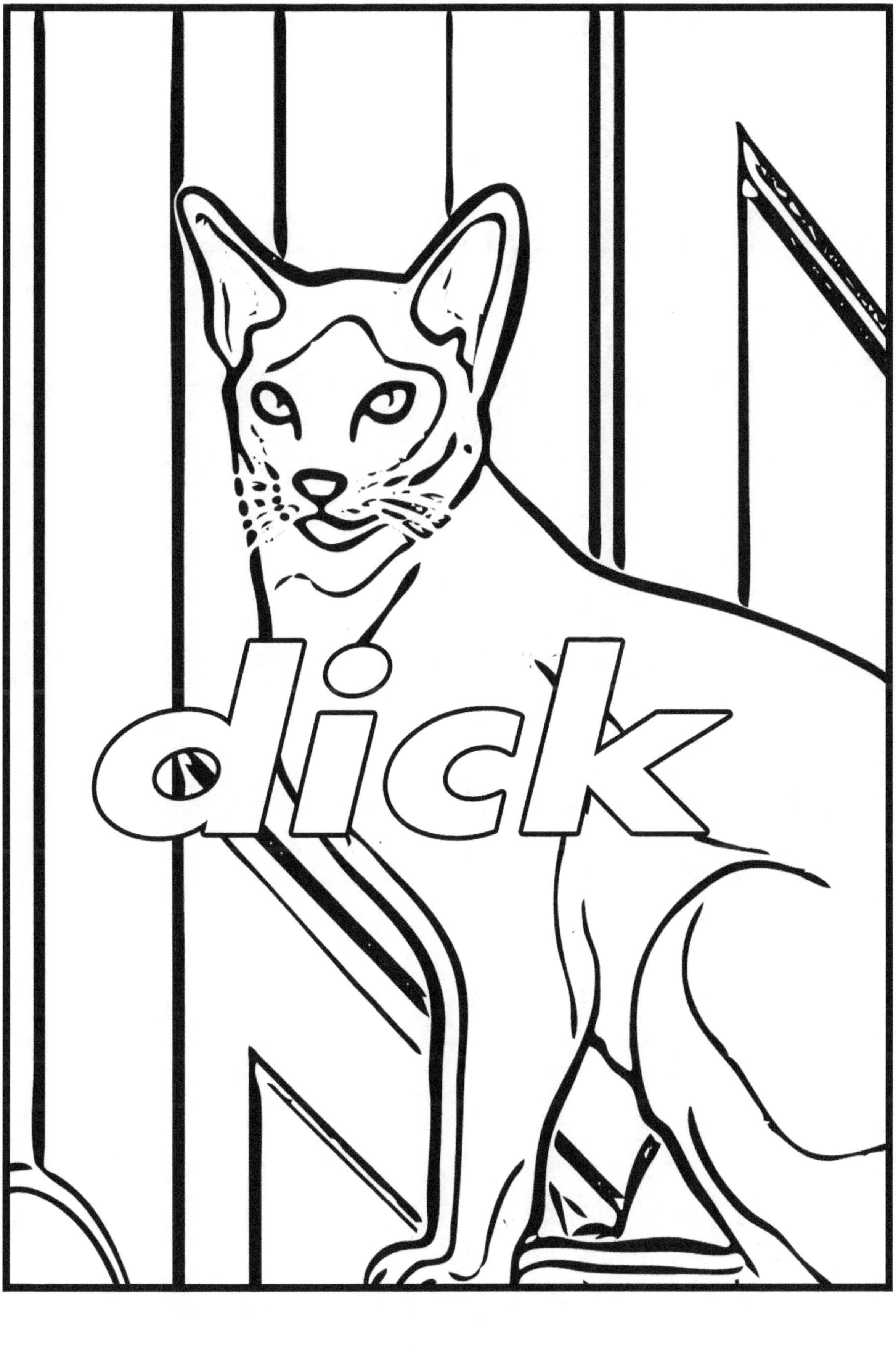
dick

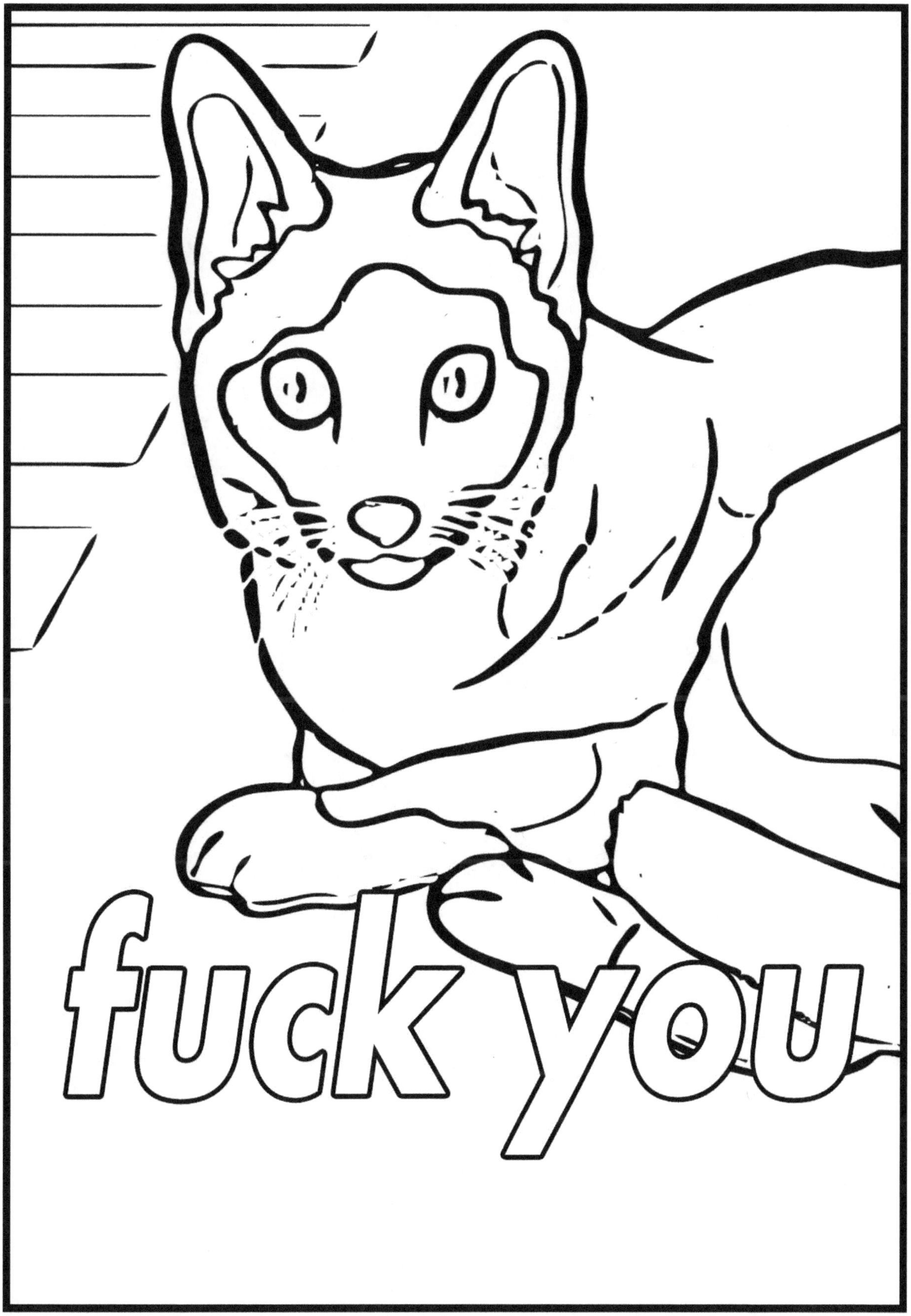
fuck you

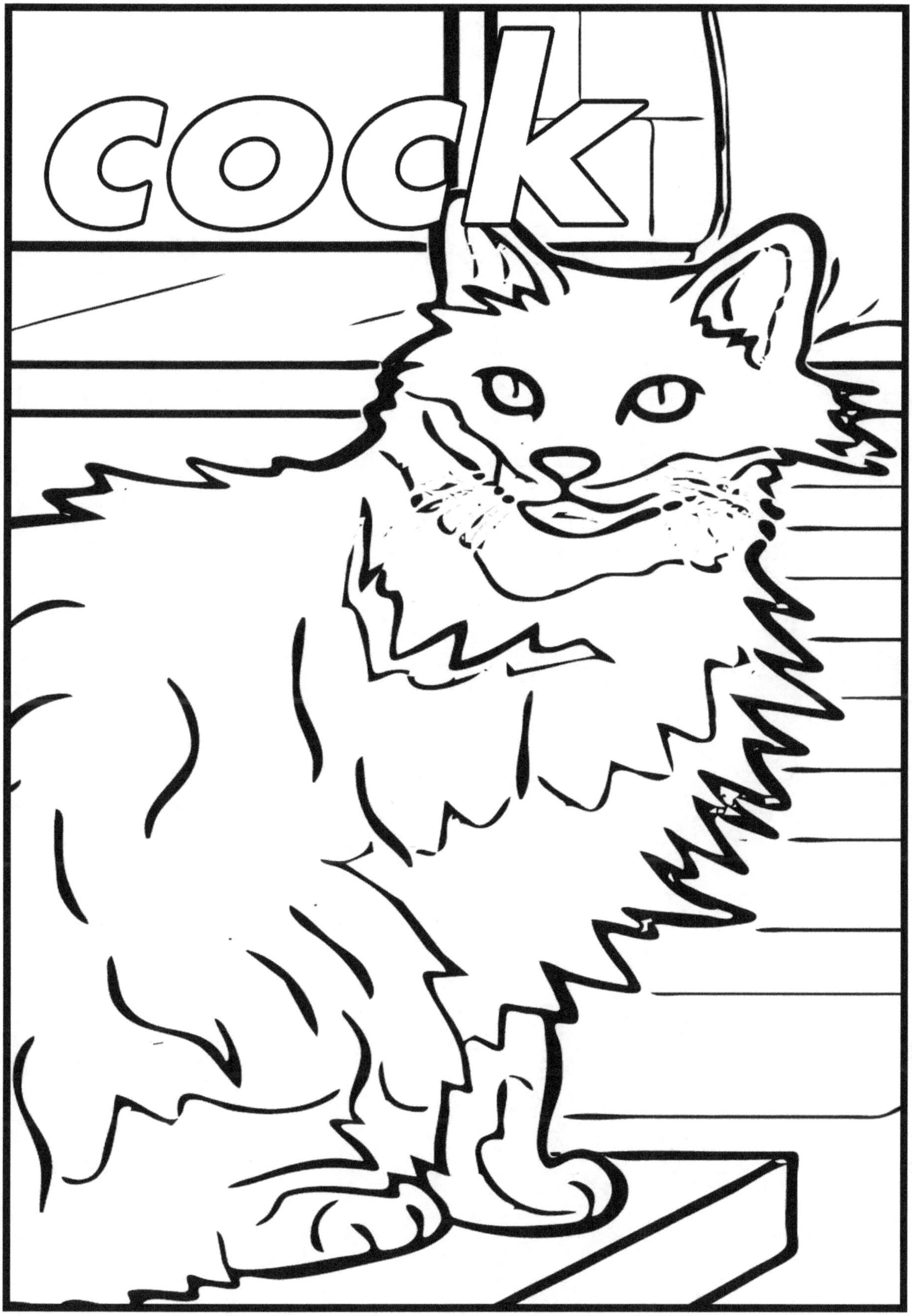
COCK

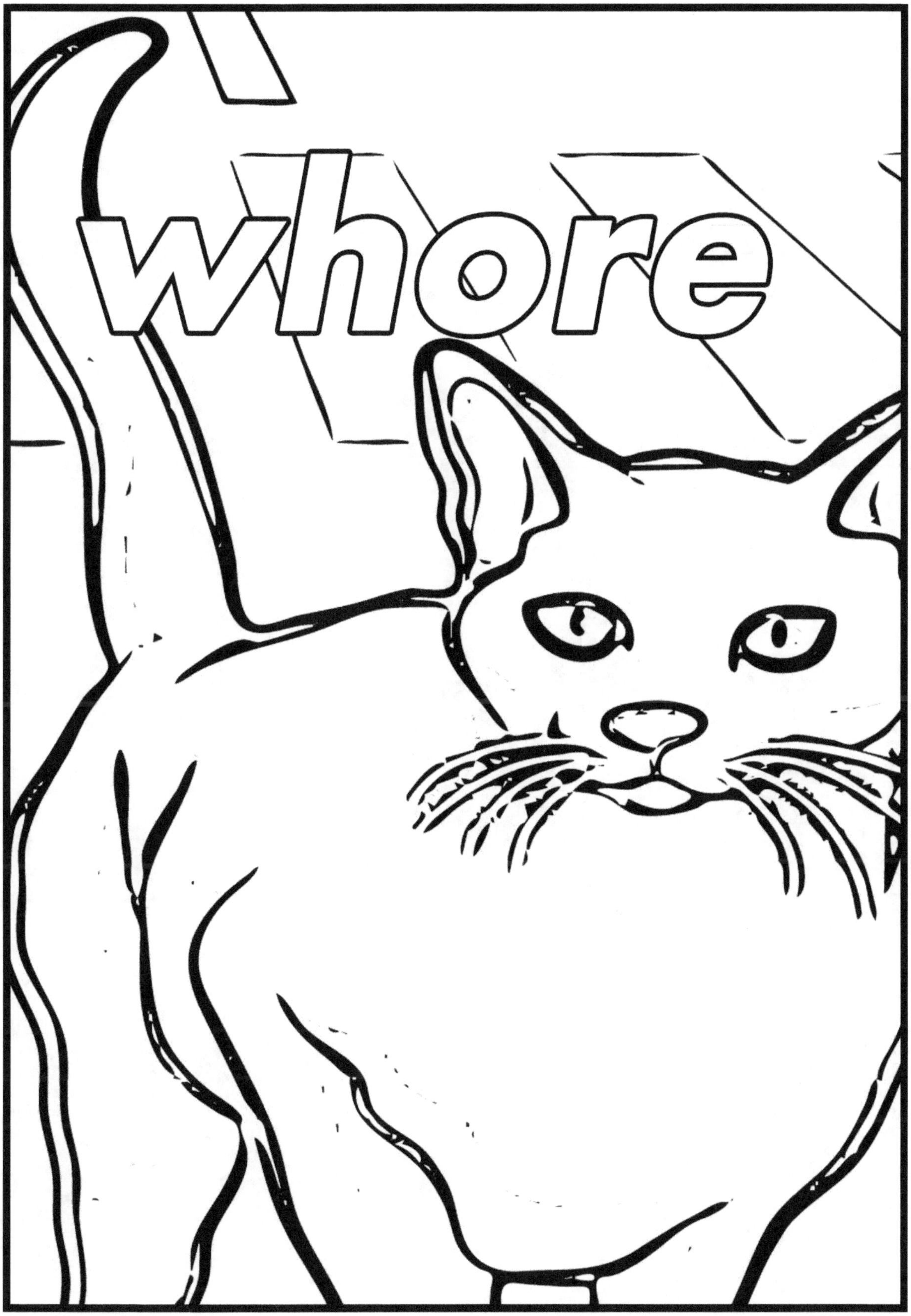
whore

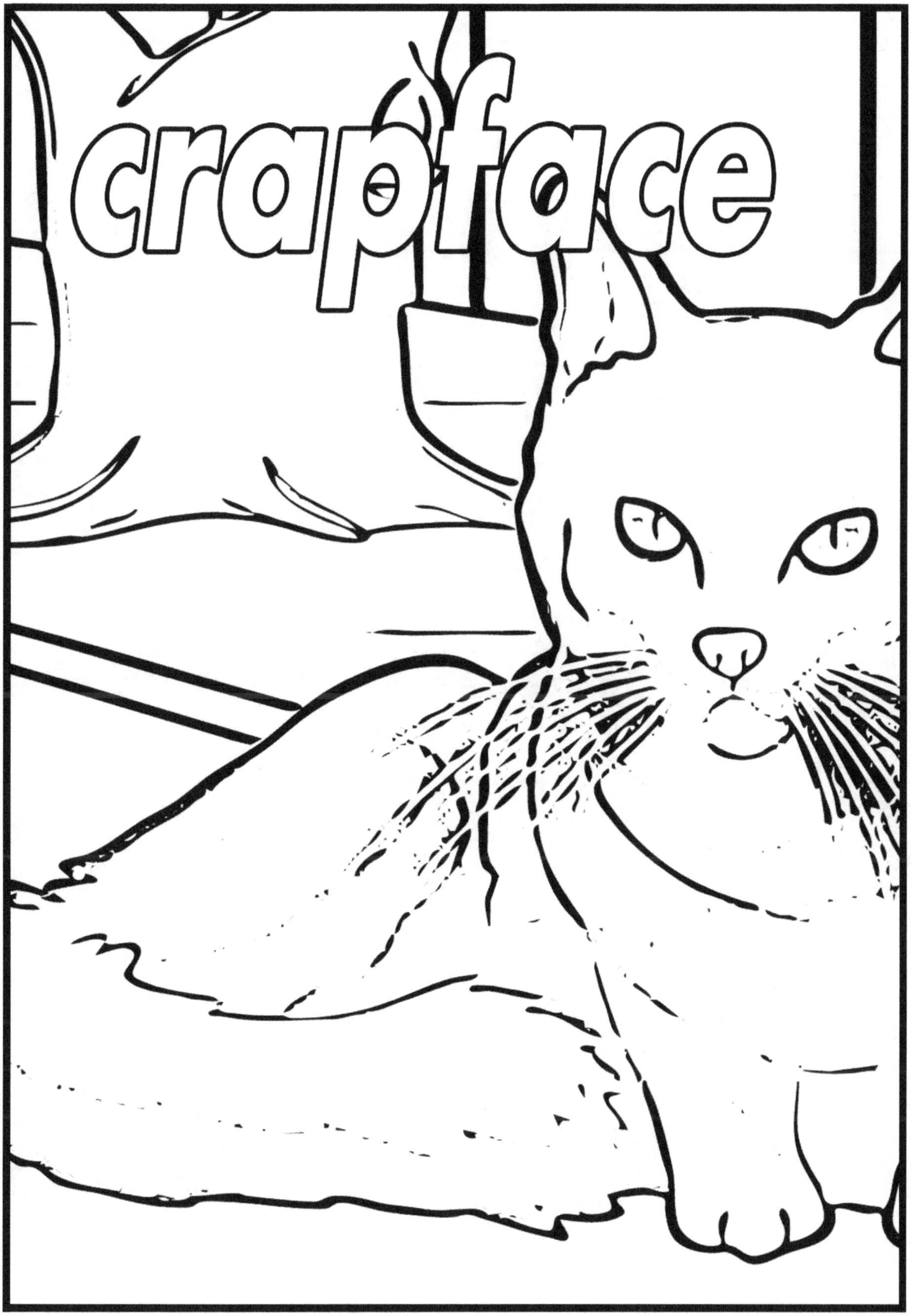
crapface

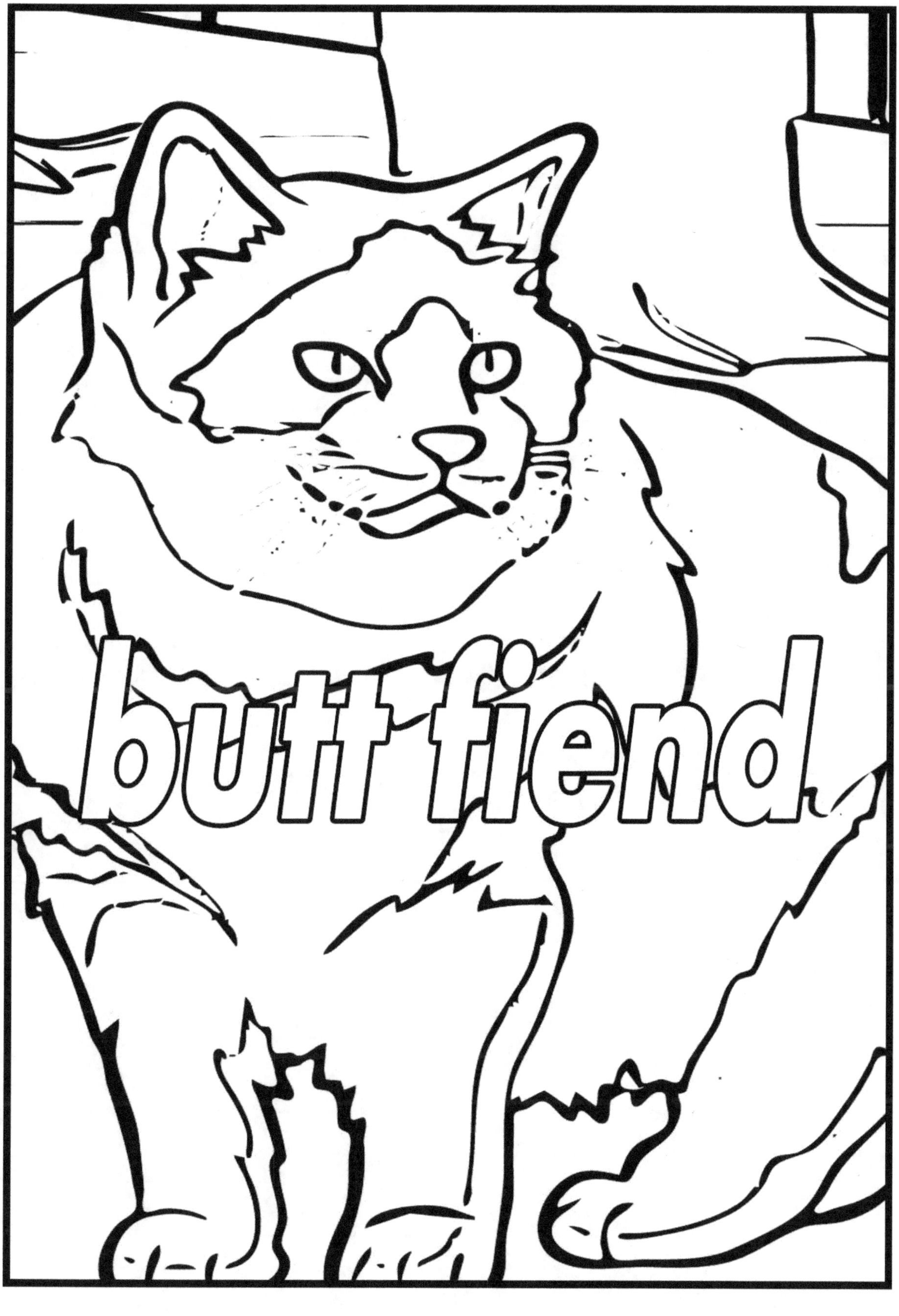
butt fiend

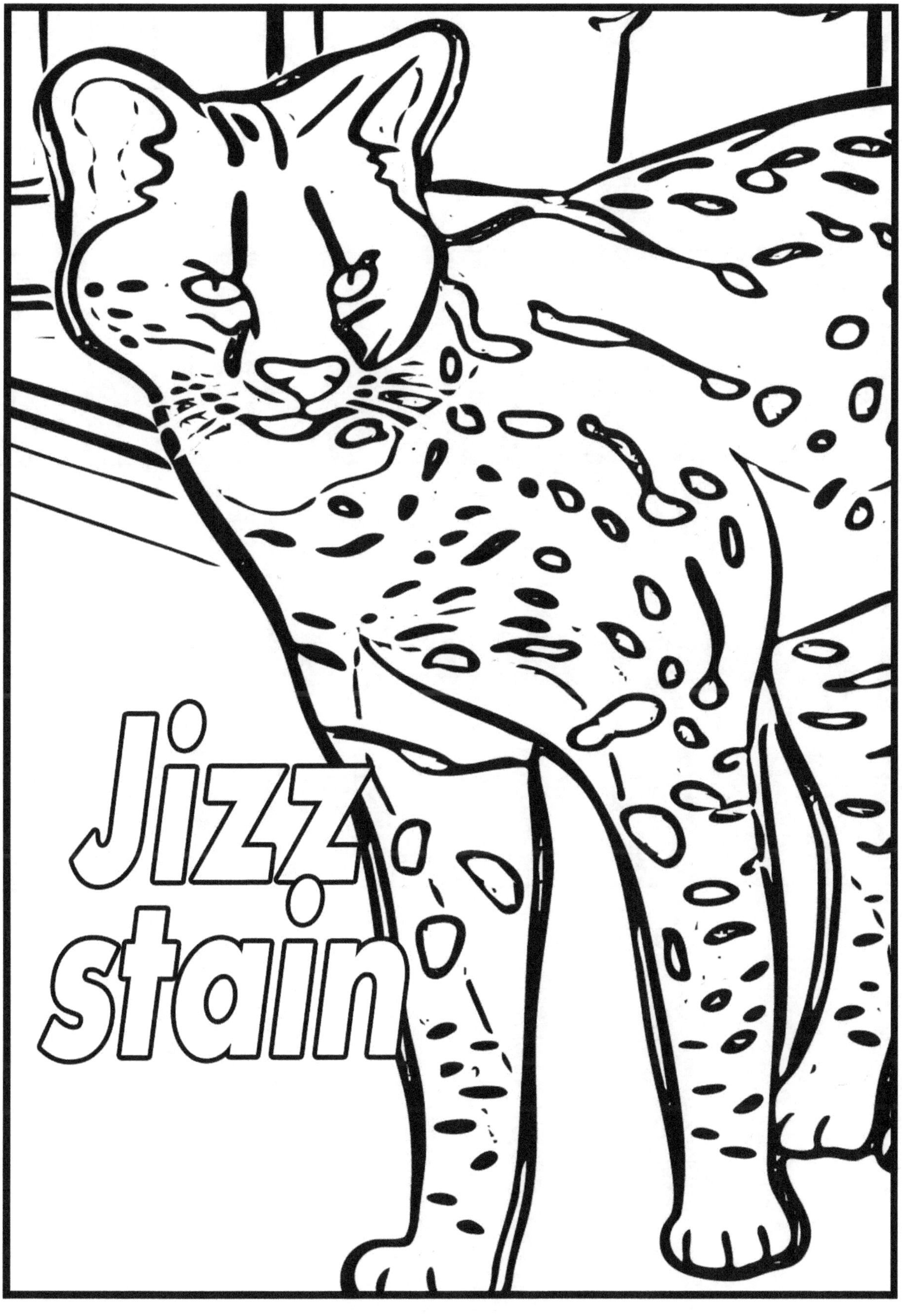
Jizz
stain

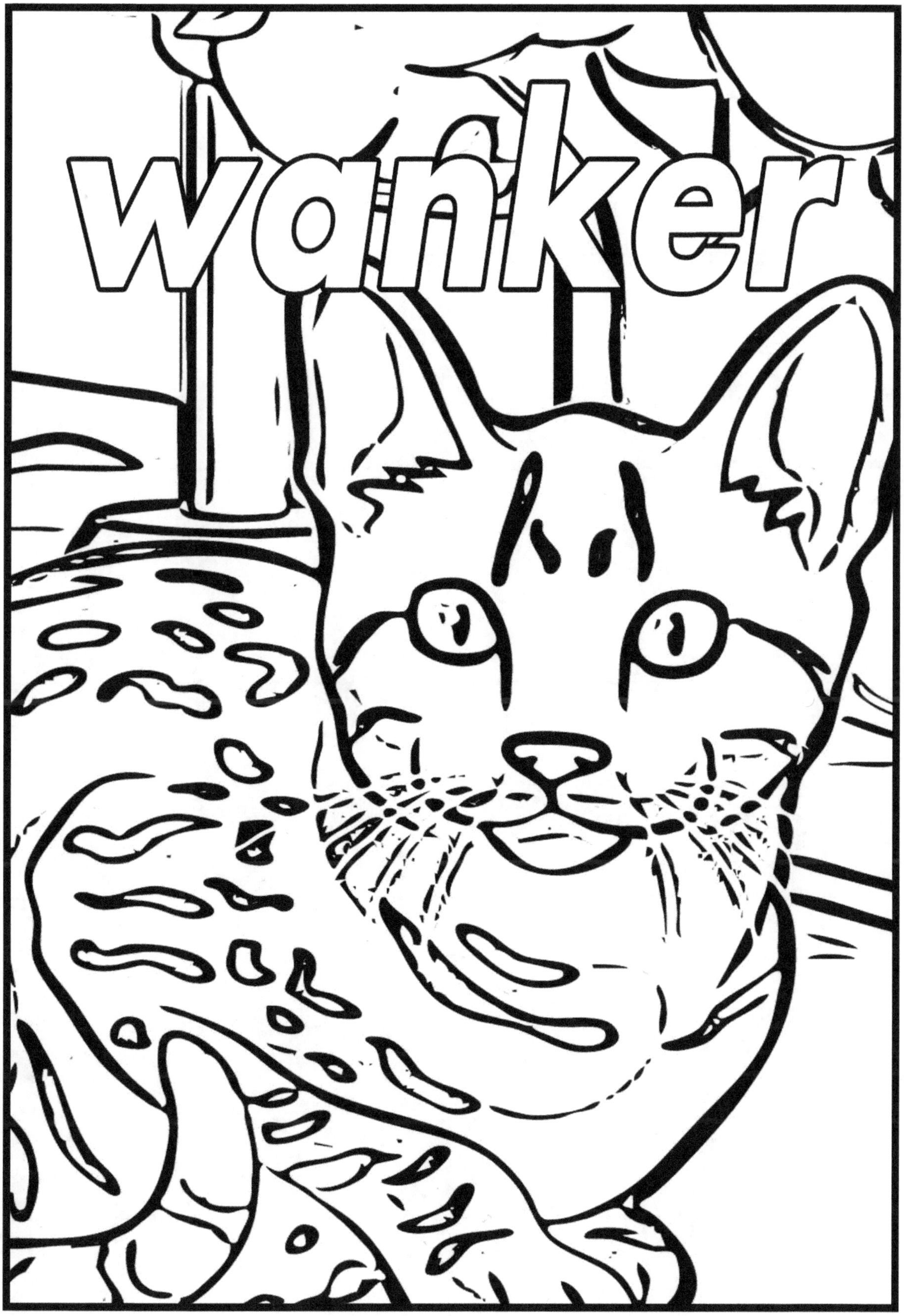
wanker

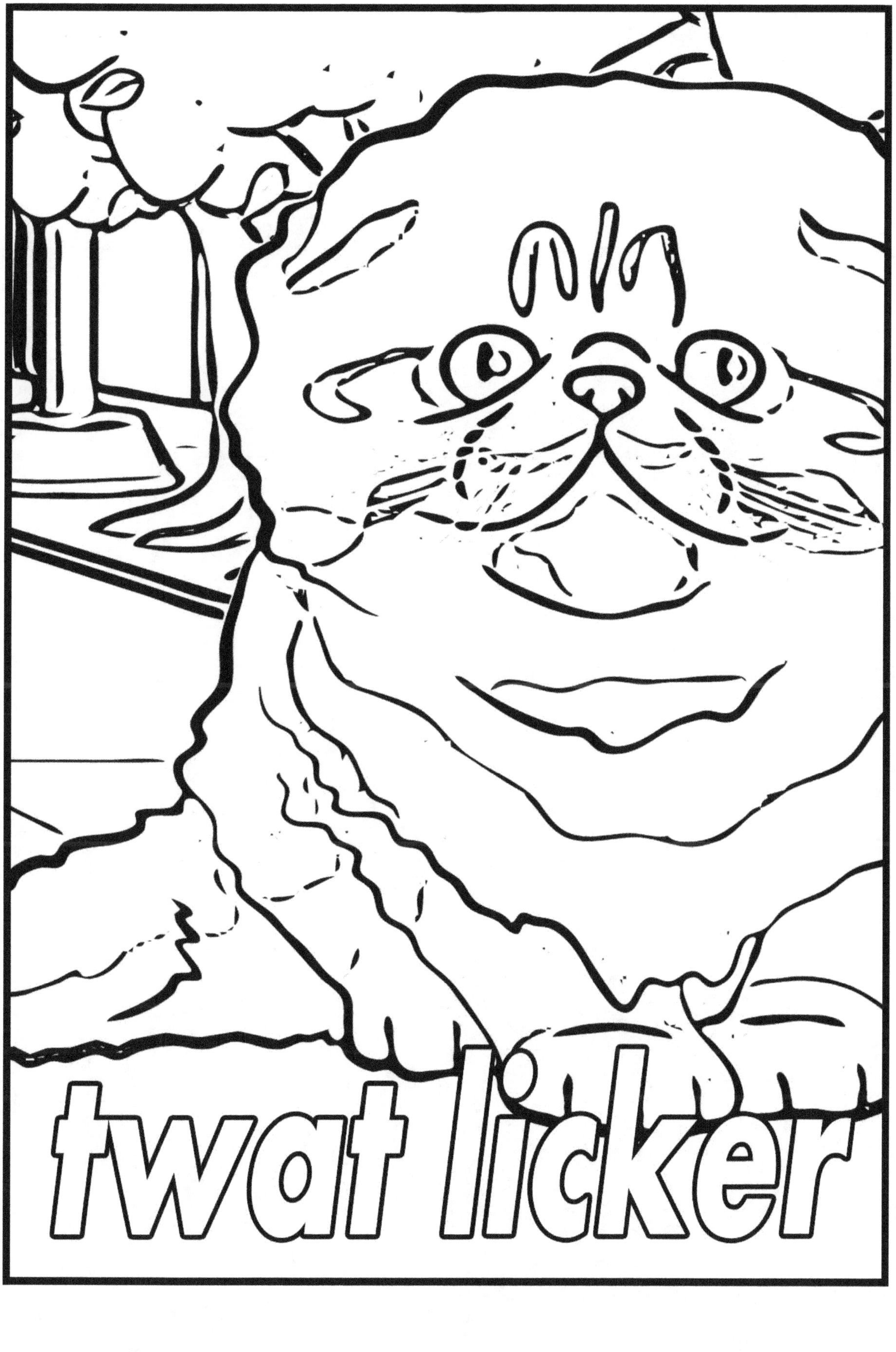
twat licker

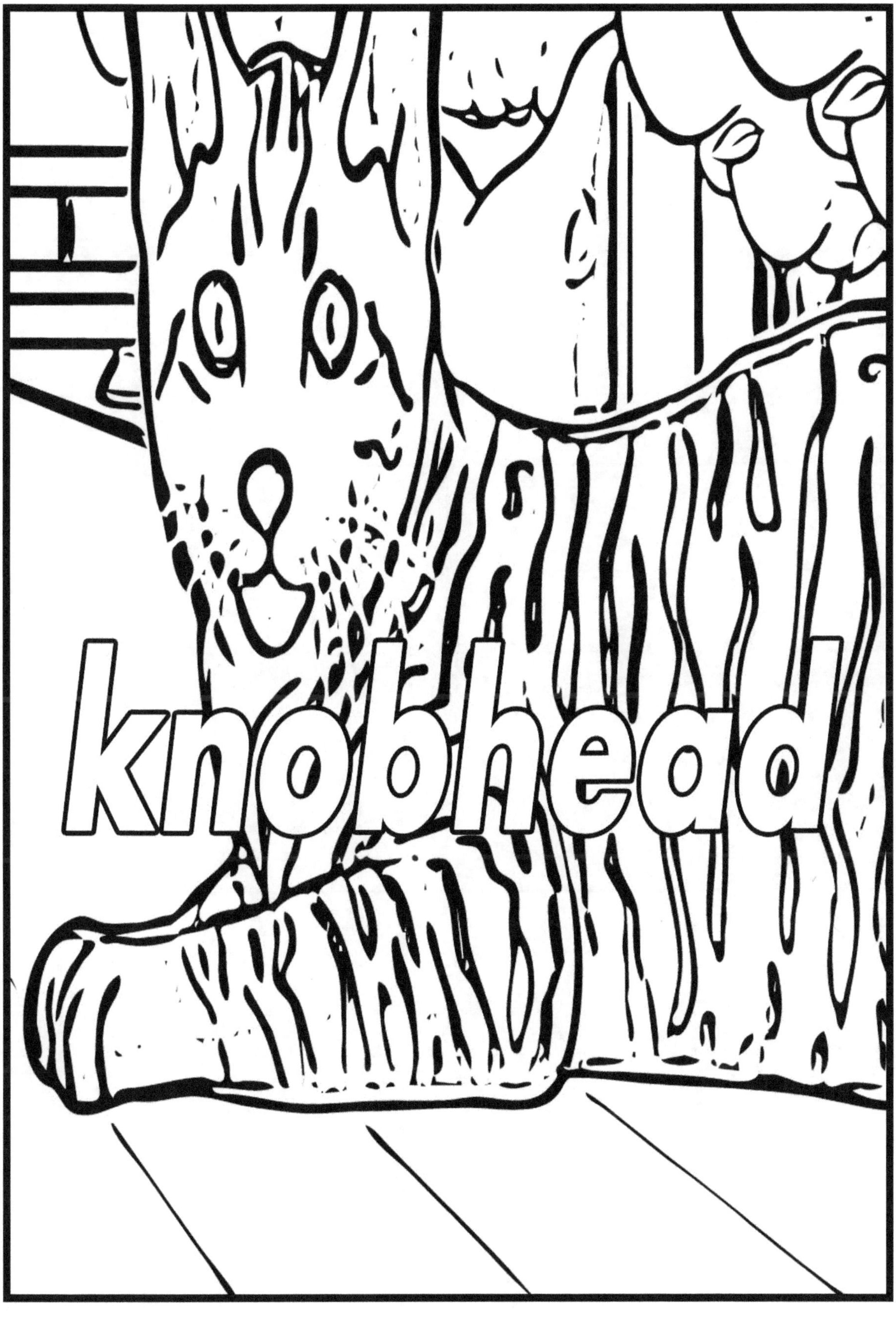
knobhead

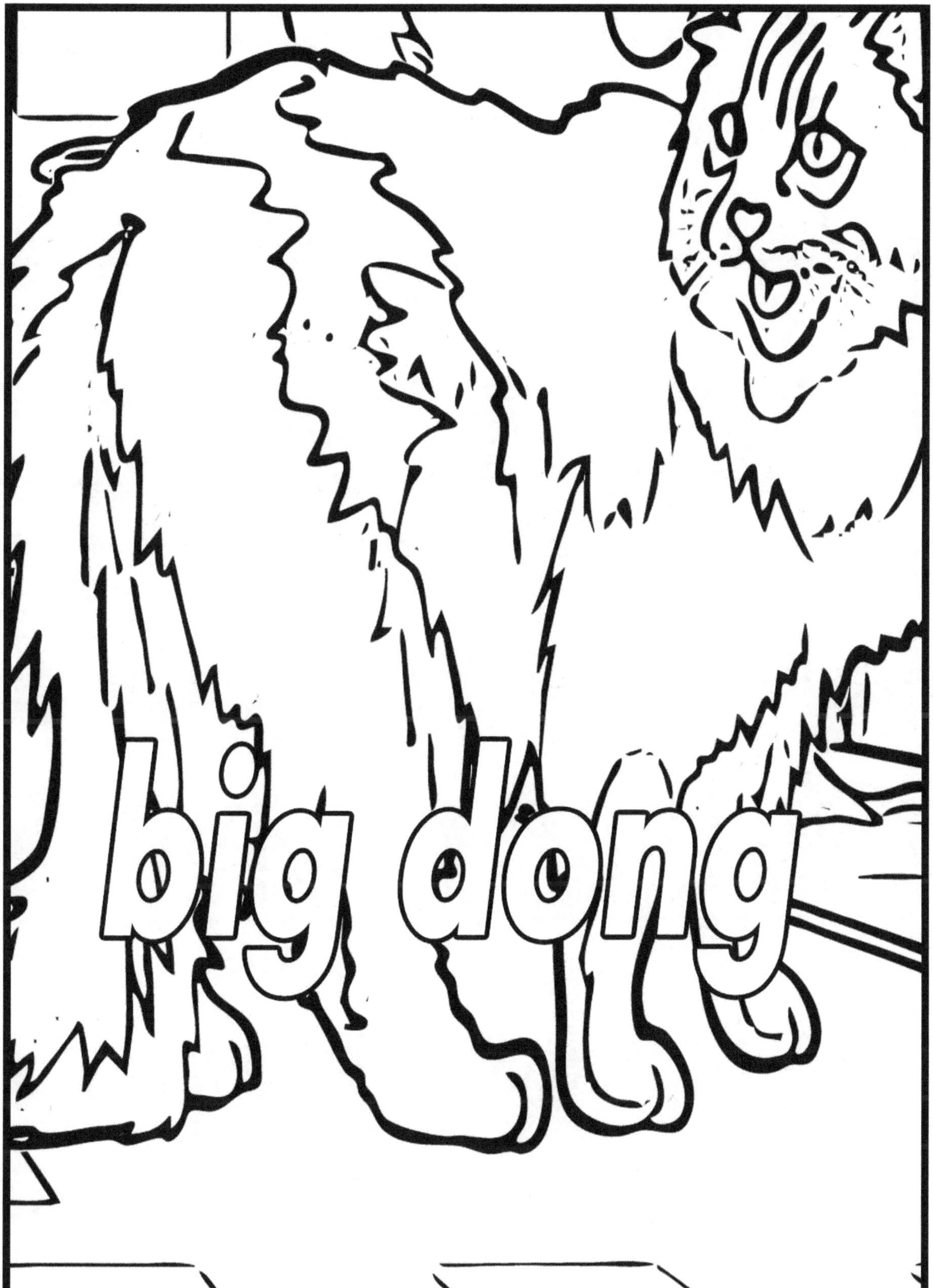
big dong

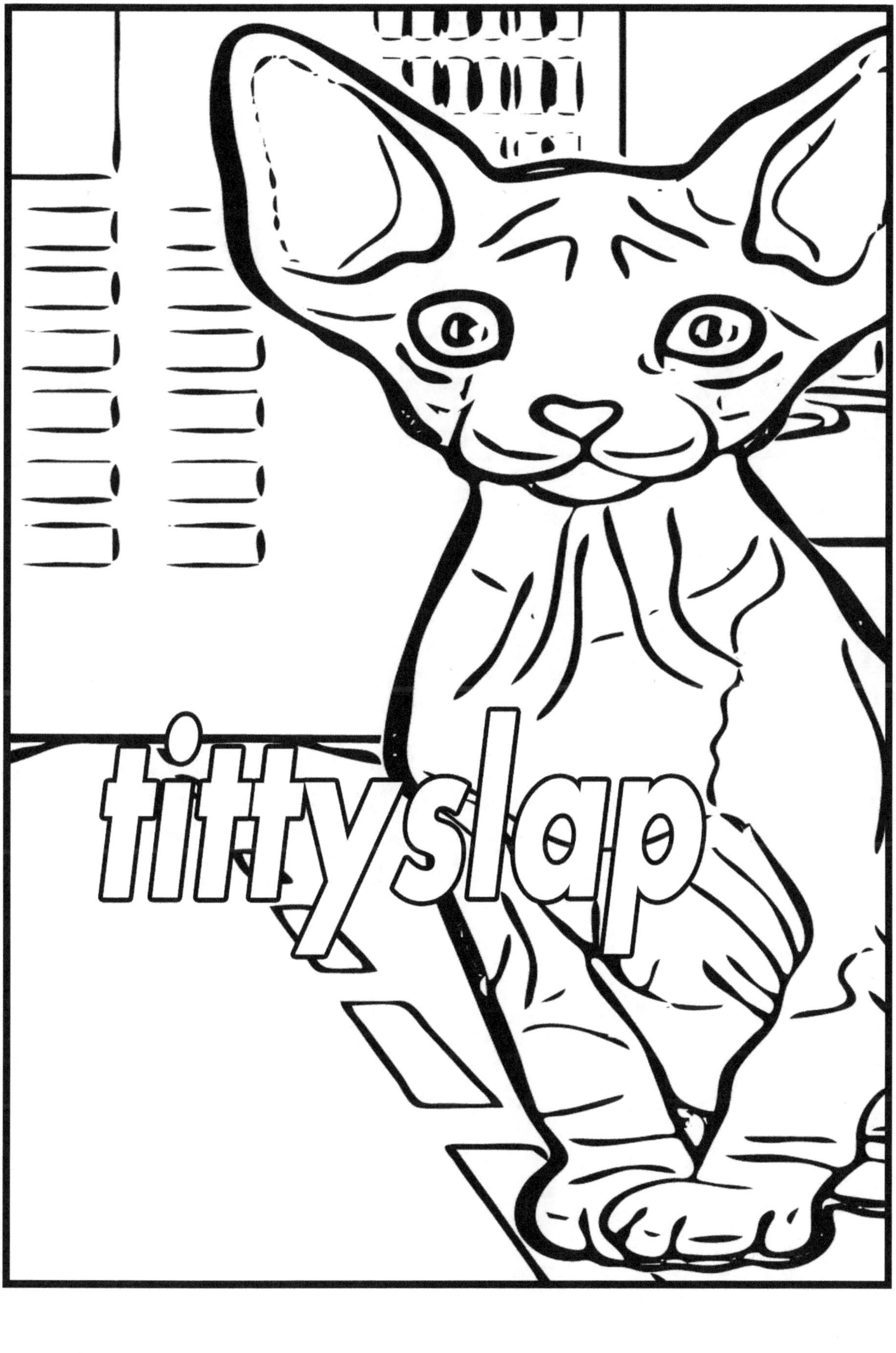
tittyslap

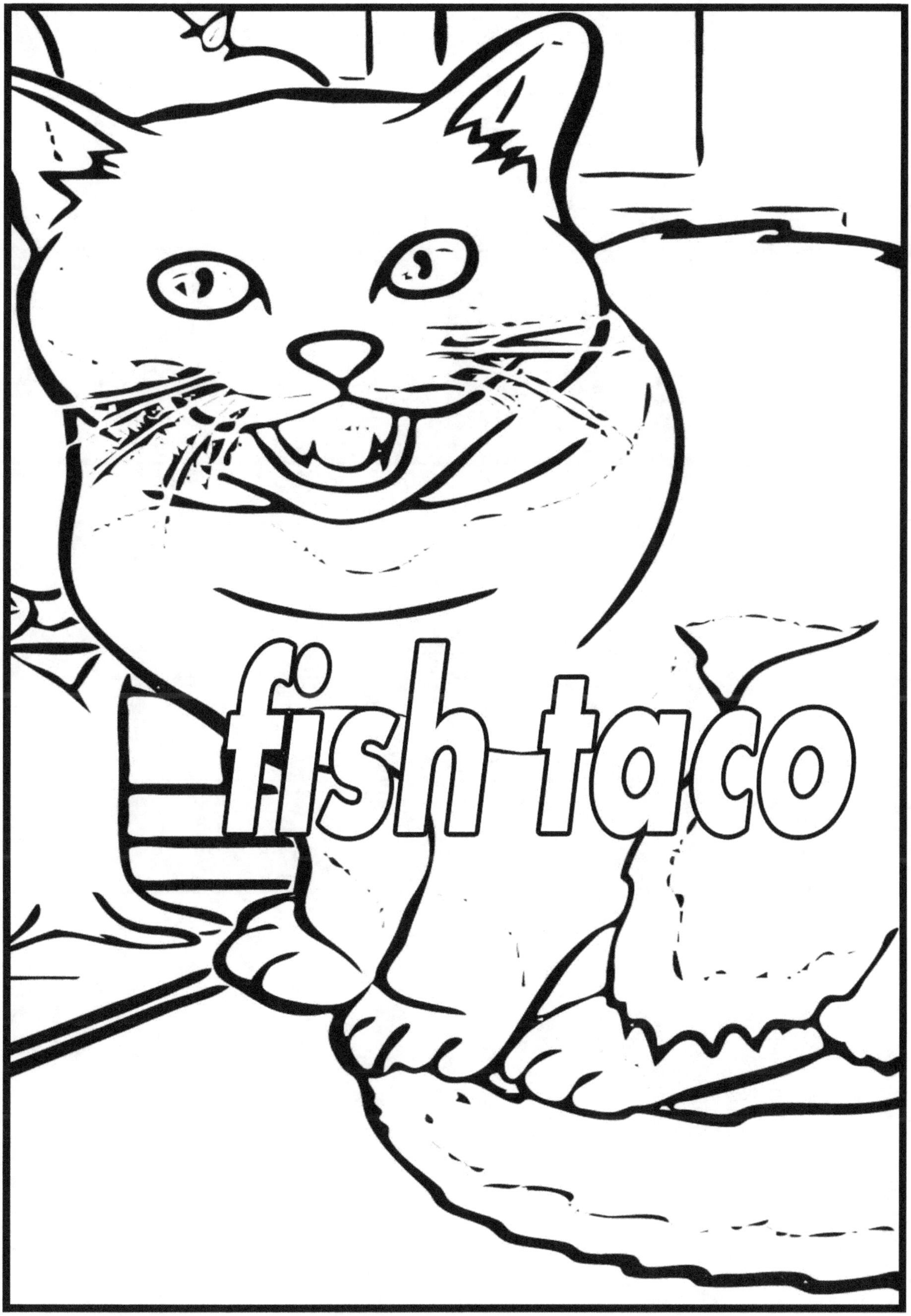
fish taco

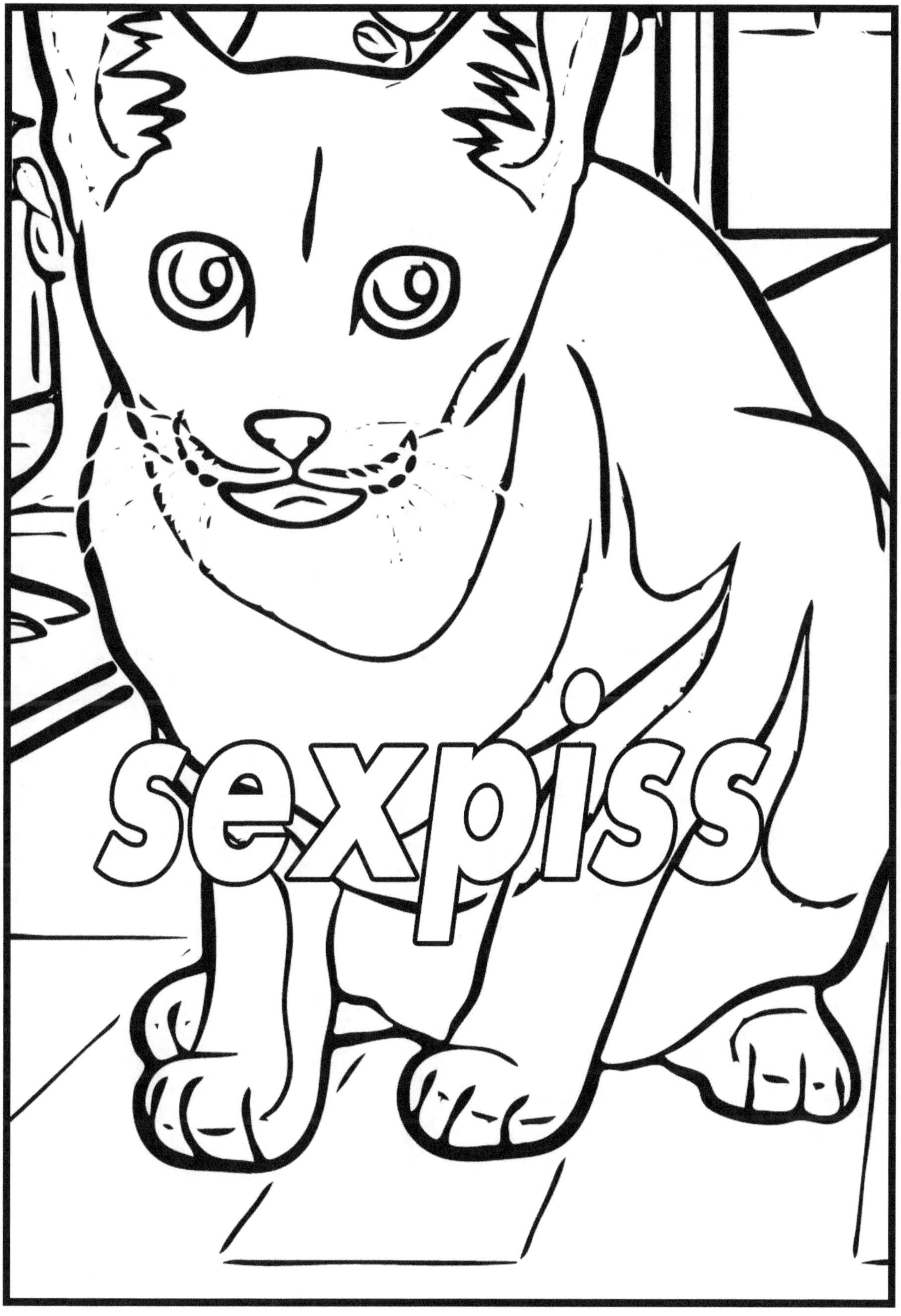
sexpiss

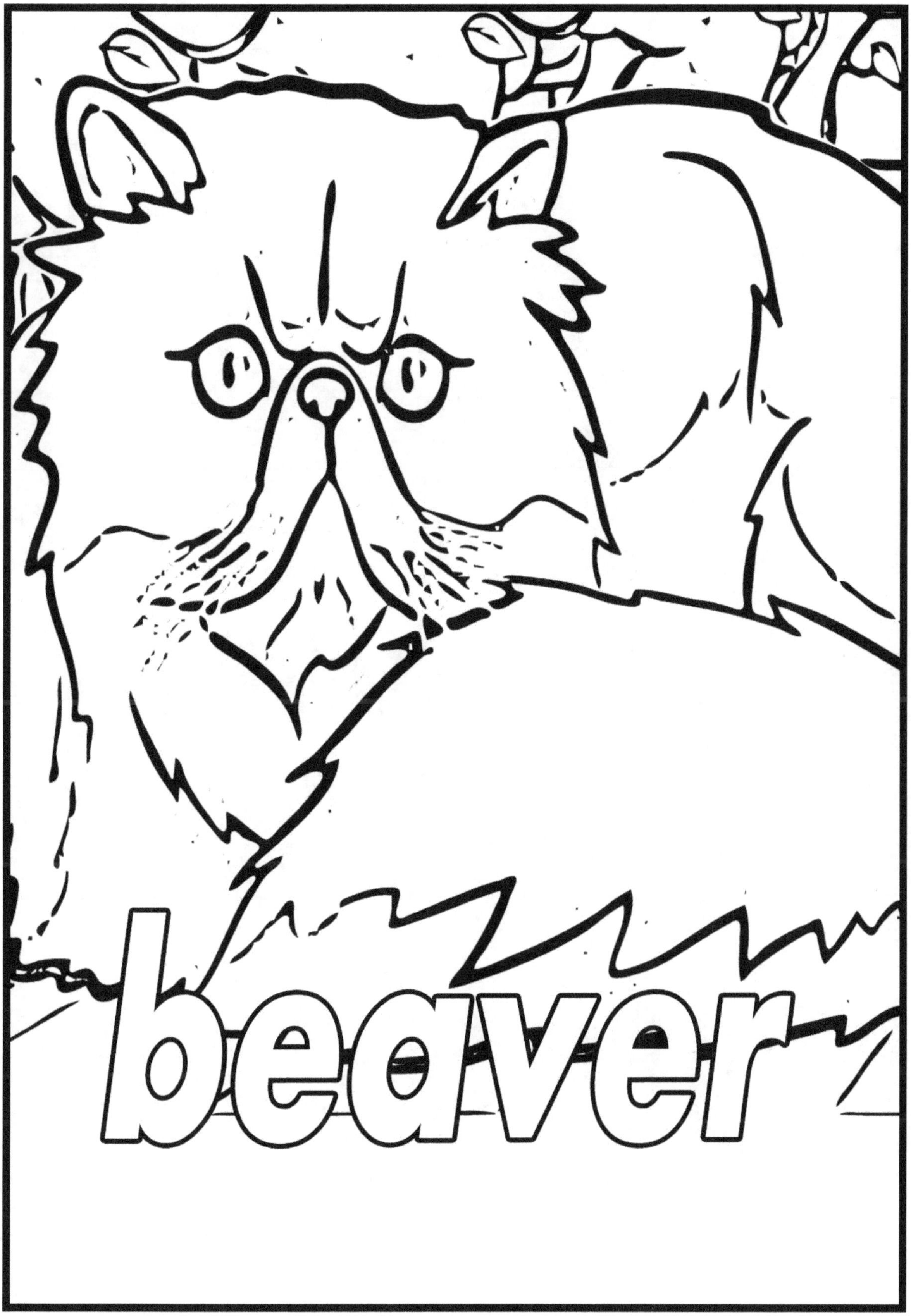
beaver

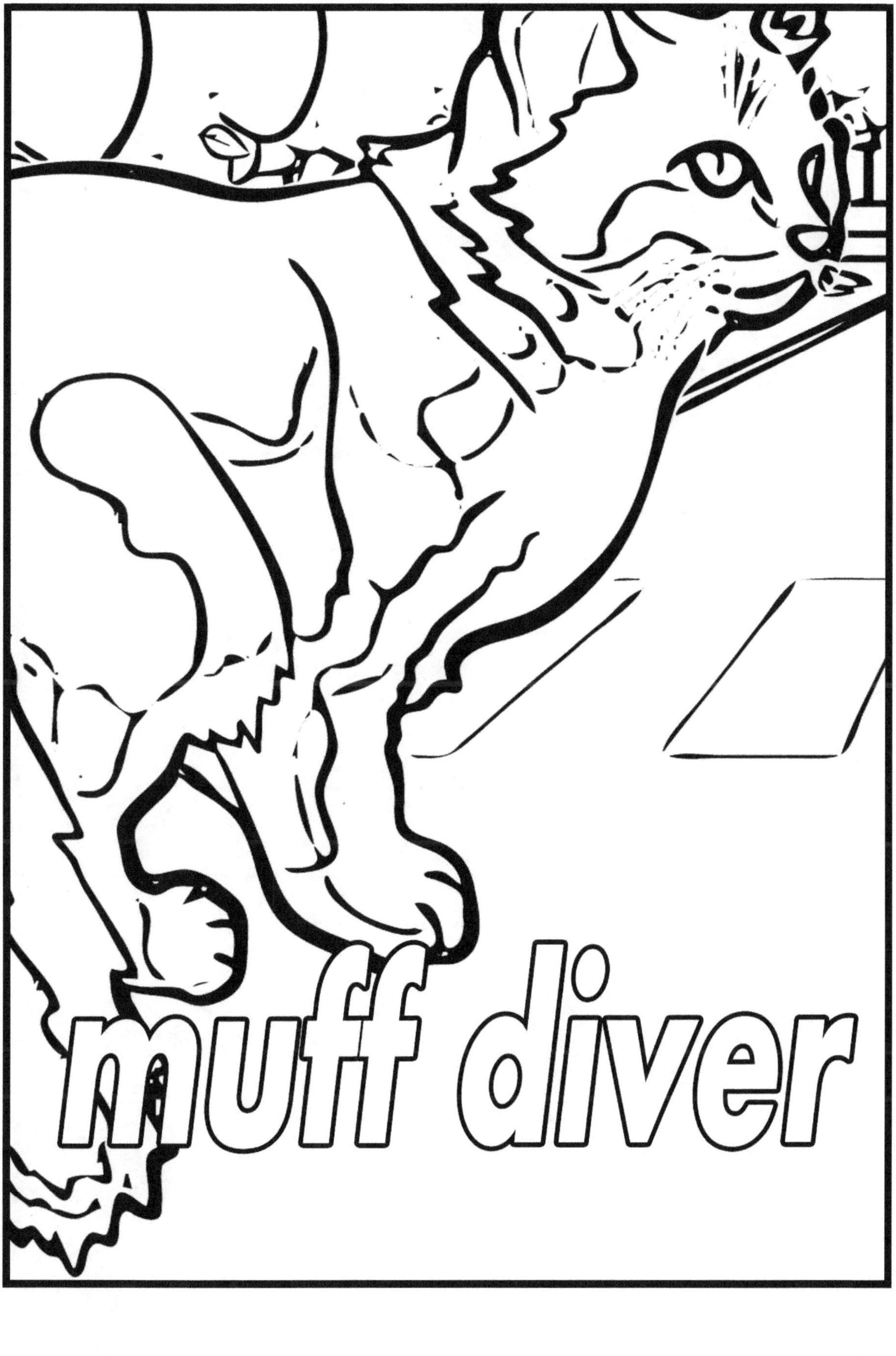
muff diver

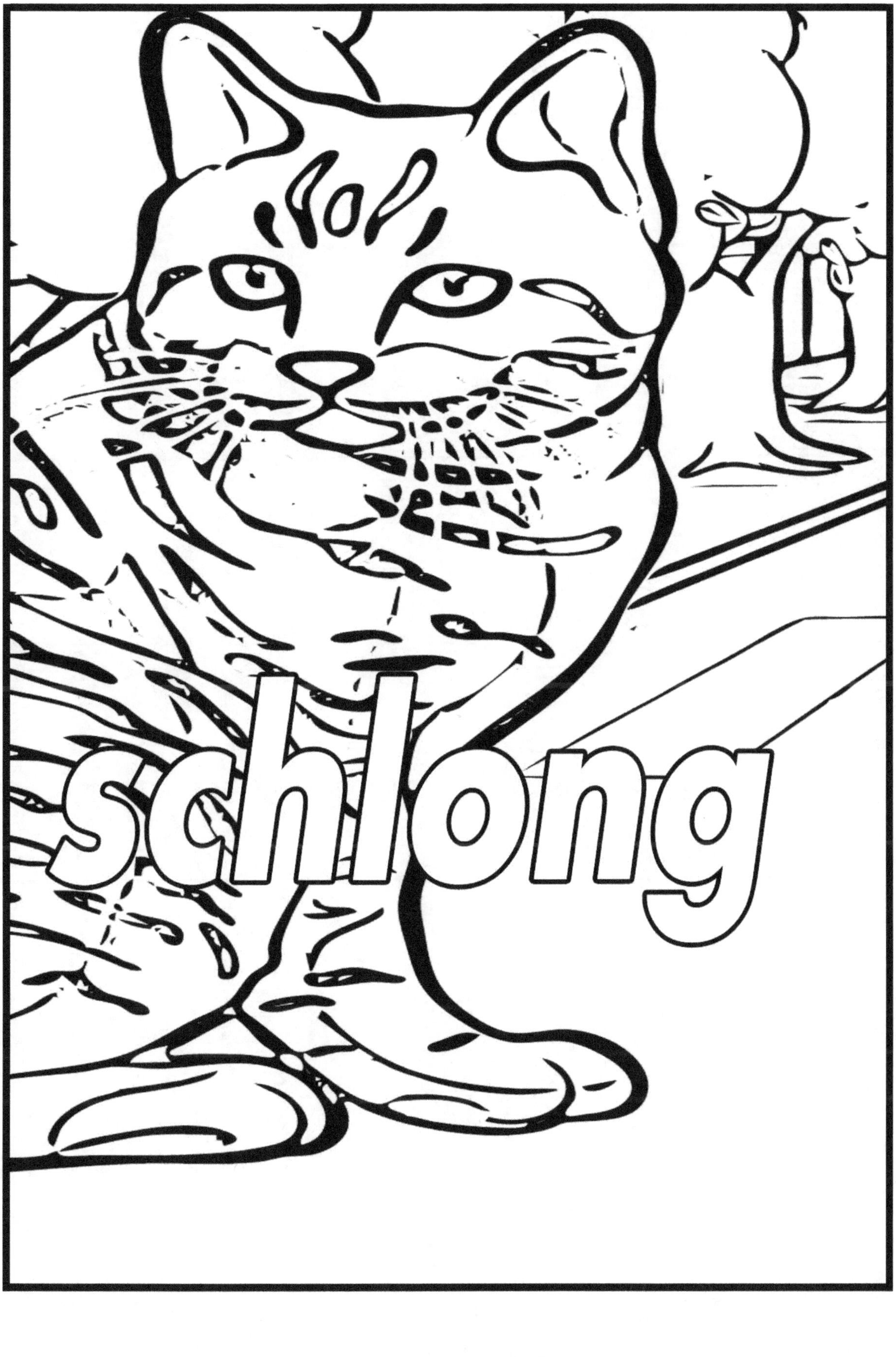
schlong

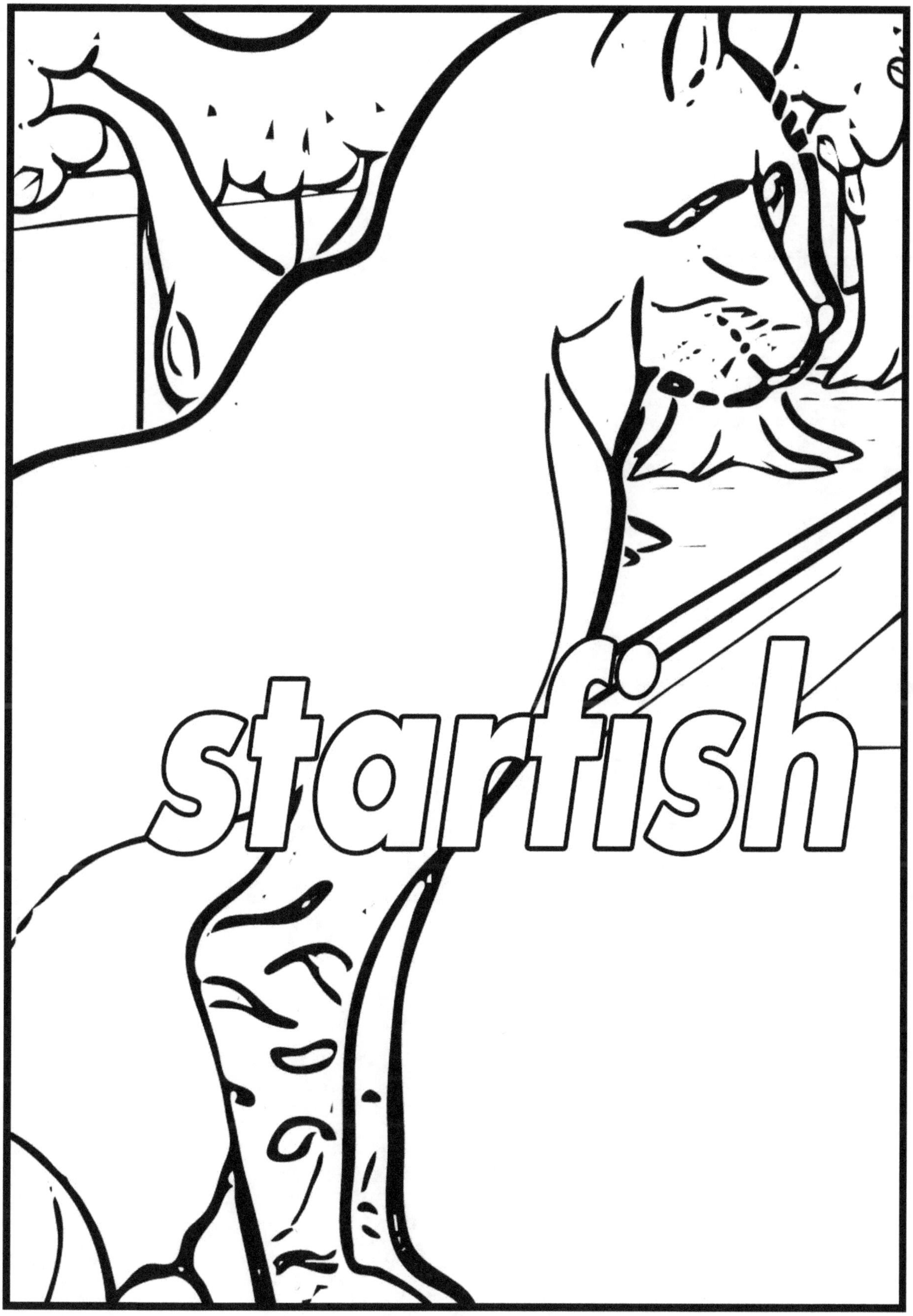
starfish

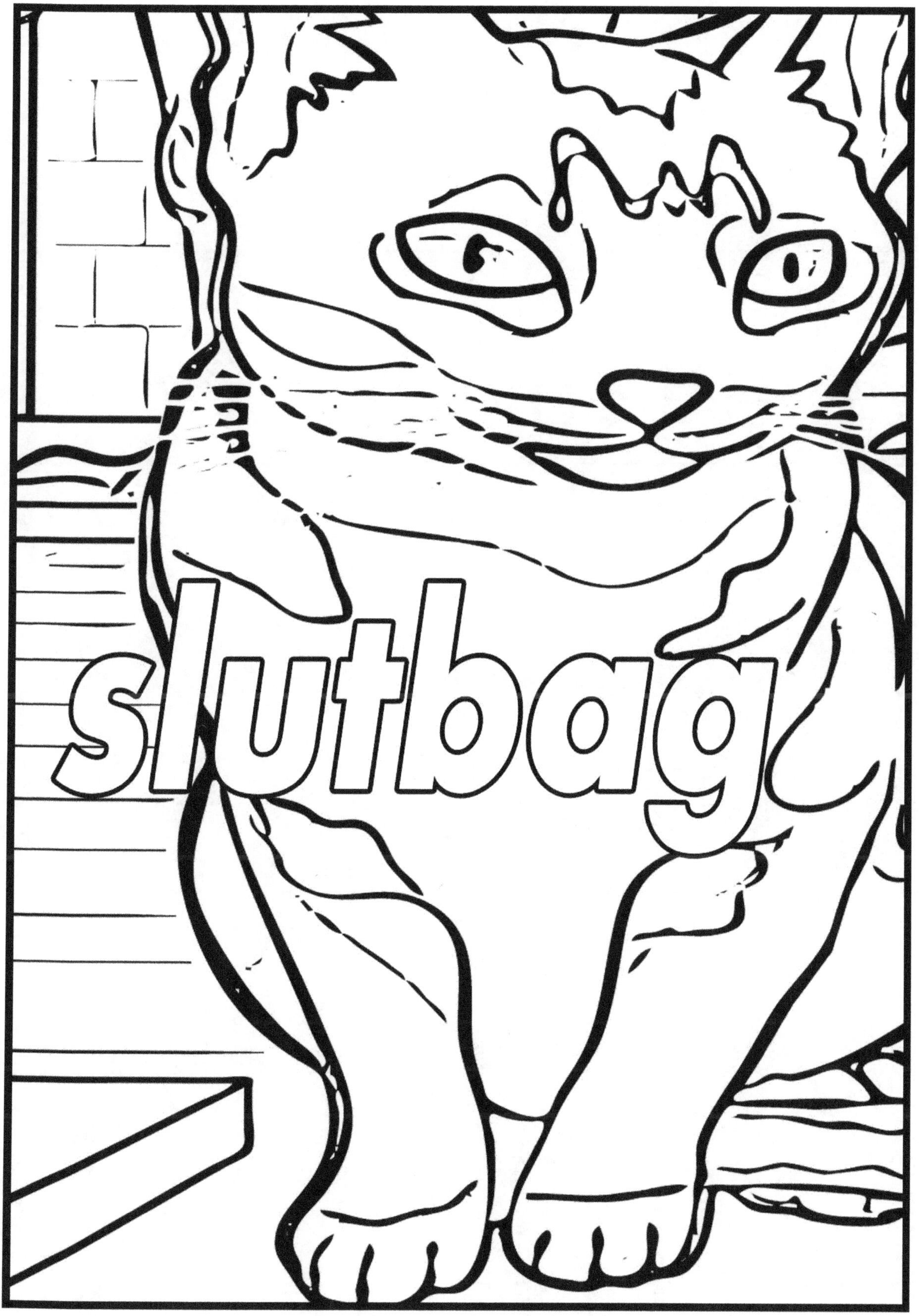
slutbag

www.ingramcontent.com/pod-product-compliance
Lightning Source LLC
Chambersburg PA
CBHW080612190526
45169CB00007B/2982
9781530204441